THE TOP TEAMS EVER

BY DALTON ROSS

A SPORTS ILLUSTRATED FOR KIDS Book

The Top Teams Ever by Dalton Ross

SPORTS ILLUSTRATED FOR KIDS and 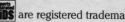 are registered trademarks of Time Inc.

Cover and interior design by Emily Peterson Perez
Cover photograph by John Biever/Sports Illustrated
Additional design by Nina Gaskin
Research by Jeff Labrecque

The Top Teams Ever is published by SPORTS ILLUSTRATED FOR KIDS, a division of Time Inc. Its trademark is registered in the U.S. Patent and Trademark Office and in other countries. SPORTS ILLUSTRATED FOR KIDS, 1271 Avenue of the Americas, New York, NY 10020

For information, address: SPORTS ILLUSTRATED FOR KIDS

ISBN 1-886749-63-9

Printed in the United States of America

10 9 8 7 6 5 4 3 2 1

The Top Teams Ever is a production of SPORTS ILLUSTRATED FOR KIDS Books:
Cathrine Wolf, Assistant Managing Editor; Emily Peterson Perez, Art Director;
Amy Lennard Goehner and Margaret Sieck (Project Editor), Senior Editors;
Scott Gramling and Sherie Holder, Associate Editors;
Robert J. Rohr, Copy Editor; Erin Tricarico, Photo Researcher;
Ron Beuzenburg, Production Manager

CONTENTS

DEDICATION

....

To Marta and Stu,
and the sisters two: Allison and Christy.
It's a family affair.

— D.R.

Introduction

What's the difference between a good team, even a very good team, and a Top Team? And with all the great teams that have lit up the world of sports, how did we pick just 10?

It wasn't easy. As you read this book, though, you will see that in each case, the teams we chose had something that made them truly special. They had something that separated them from the pack.

In some cases, that something was a player unlike any other. Michael Jordan lifted the Chicago Bulls to another, higher level of excellence. Wayne Gretzky did the same thing for the Edmonton Oilers.

In other cases, a different style of play set the team apart. The 1960's Boston Celtics' fast break and the 1980's San Francisco 49ers' "West Coast offense" are examples of that.

For some teams, it was simply an astonishing collection of raw talent — like that of the Montreal Canadiens and the Cincinnati Reds. Still other teams, such as the 1998 New York Yankees, were able to win so many games that their greatness could not be denied.

In any event, whenever opponents faced the teams in this book, they knew they weren't facing "just another team." They were facing one of *The Top Teams Ever*.

1

THE DENVER BRONCOS

· · · · · · · · · · · · · · · · · · ·

After years of frustration, John Elway and company find Super Bowl success

The road to the top is never smooth. Nobody knows that better than the Denver Broncos.

Quarterback John Elway took the Broncos to the Super Bowl in 1987, 1988, and 1990. They lost all three games. They lost by a lot. First they fell to the New York Giants, 39–20. Then the Washington Redskins beat them 42–10. The San Francisco 49ers killed them 55–10, in 1990.

Experts knew that John was one of the best quarterbacks in football. But people started to wonder if his team would ever win The Big One. Maybe John was one of those players who just could not win big games. Or maybe he just didn't have enough gifted teammates around him. Either way, for

John and the Broncos, it was frustrating. It was almost embarrassing!

Then a new coach and a dynamite running back arrived. Before long, the Broncos were one of the best teams in NFL history. Best of all, they were Super Bowl champions! Denver won 33 of 39 games (including playoffs and the Super Bowl) and back-to-back championships in 1998 and 1999.

NEW FACES IN THE RIGHT PLACES

Denver's march to Super Bowl success began in 1995. The team made several important decisions that year, which helped them win the Super Bowl later.

First, they hired Mike Shanahan as head coach. He had helped the San Francisco 49ers win their fifth Super Bowl in 1995 as the team's offensive coordinator. He also knew the Broncos. He had been one of the team's offensive coaches from 1984 to 1987 and from 1989 to 1991. In addition, he and John were good friends.

Coach Shanahan liked to create complicated plays to confuse the other team. But when it came to dealing with his players, he liked to keep things simple and direct. "To me, the bottom line is that people trust you," Coach Shanahan said. "They might not like what you have to say, but if you're honest and treat them like men, I think they respect you." The Denver players respected Coach Shanahan.

The Broncos filled in another piece of the championship puzzle at the 1995 NFL draft. They selected running back Terrell Davis in the sixth round. Terrell had been injured as a senior at the University of Georgia. Some teams thought he was too slow for the NFL. As a result, 20 running backs were chosen by other teams before Terrell. Guess what? Terrell ended up being the best player in the whole draft!

Terrell was 5' 11" and 205 pounds. He was quick and powerful. He tore up the NFL from the moment he played his first game. He ran for 1,117 yards on 237 carries as a Bronco rookie in 1995. That made him the lowest-drafted player in NFL history to rush for 1,000 yards in a season. In 1996, he ran for a team-record 1,538 yards on 345 carries. Only superstar Barry Sanders of the Detroit Lions rushed for more yards that season!

Denver had never had a great running back like Terrell to team with John. Now, they finally had one.

Two other key players joined the Broncos in 1995: wide receivers Ed McCaffrey and Rod Smith. Ed was a big, tall target for John. He could catch any ball thrown in his direction. Rod combined great speed and leaping ability. Over the next four seasons, Ed and Rod combined for 5,464 yards and 48 touchdowns. The Broncos already had the NFL's best tight end, Shannon Sharpe. Now, with Rod and Ed, their passing game was unstoppable.

In 1995, Denver had an 8–8 record as the new coach, new players, and veterans got used to one another. The next season, the Broncos were awesome!

They cruised to a 13–3 regular-season record — the best in the American Football Conference (AFC). They looked like strong Super Bowl contenders. But some of the players got too confident. They assumed that they would win their first playoff game against the Jacksonville Jaguars, a wild-card team. That was a mistake. The Jaguars came into Denver's Mile High Stadium and upset the Broncos, 30–27!

MILE HIGH SALUTES

Had Denver blown its big chance to win the NFL championship? That was one of the questions facing the Broncos when the 1997 season began.

And what about John? John had had surgery on his right shoulder in the off-season. He recovered but then hurt his right bicep in a pre-season game. Nobody was sure if he would be able to throw the ball well. John is right-handed.

All those questions were answered when Denver took the field for its first game of 1997. John proved that his arm was as good as ever. He threw a 78-yard bomb to Rod and finished with 246 yards as the Broncos beat the Kansas City Chiefs, 19–3. After victories over the Seattle Seahawks and St. Louis Rams, the Broncos faced the Cincinnati Bengals.

Terrell had run for more than 100 yards in each of the first three games but had saved his best for the Bengals. He rushed for 215 yards and a touchdown in 27 carries. That made him the first Bronco ever to run for more than 200 yards in a game! When Terrell scored on a 50-yard touchdown run in the fourth quarter, the Denver players showed off a new move: the Mile High Salute. The Denver running backs had begun calling themselves the No Limit Soldiers in training camp because they believed that there was no limit to what they could accomplish on the field. So the "soldiers" started saluting themselves when they scored.

After the 38–20 victory over Cincinnati, even Coach Shanahan saluted Terrell, in the locker room. "I can't figure out what it means," the coach admitted. "But it's working, so I'm saluting."

DOING IT THE HARD WAY

Everything the Broncos did in 1997 seemed to work. They raced to a terrific 9–1 record. John was playing better than ever. So was the rest of the Bronco offense. They were nearly unstoppable.

Late in the season, though, the Broncos ran into trouble. They lost three of their last six games and ended the season with a 12–4 record. That made them a wild-card team in the playoffs. Wild-card teams have to win an extra game to

SIMPLY PERFECT

You win some, you lose some, right? Not for the 1972 Miami Dolphins. They won them all!

The '72 Dolphins are the only team ever to go all the way through an NFL season without a loss or tie. They won all 14 regular-season games (the NFL season was shorter). Then they won three straight in the playoffs to capture the 1973 Super Bowl and finish with an unmatched 17–0 record.

On offense, the Dolphins were led by quarterbacks Bob Griese [GREE-see] and Earl Morrall. At running back, they had Larry Csonka [ZONK-a]. Larry was as strong as a bull, which made him very difficult to tackle.

Miami's defense called itself the "No-Name Defense," because it did not have any flashy personalities or big stars. But it did have a lot of great players. One of the best was middle linebacker and team leader Nick Buoniconti [be-YON-i-CON-ti].

The Dolphins capped their stunning season by defeating the Washington Redskins, 14–7, in Super Bowl VII. A year later, they became the first team to play in three straight Super Bowls and won their second title.

But 1972 was the best. For Miami and its fans, it was perfect.

make it to the Super Bowl. Only one wild-card team had ever won the Super Bowl: the 1980 Oakland Raiders.

But the Broncos were determined to avenge their 1996 playoff disaster. They met the Jacksonville Jaguars again in their first playoff game. This time, the Broncos were ready. John led Denver on three long touchdown drives before the Jaguars even got a first down! When the dust settled, the Broncos had crushed Jacksonville, 42–17.

Still, Denver had to win twice more on the road to get to the 1998 Super Bowl. First up was a trip to play the Kansas City Chiefs. Nobody was more excited about it than Bronco defensive end Neil Smith. Neil, age 31, had played nine of his NFL seasons with the Chiefs. But Kansas City felt Neil's best years were behind him. He signed as a free agent with Denver in April of 1997.

Now Neil was on a mission. He wanted to show the Chiefs that giving up on him had been a big mistake. In the game, he sacked Chief quarterback Elvis Grbac *[GUR-back]* twice and forced a fumble. Mission accomplished.

John was his usual terrific self, passing for 170 yards. Denver won, 14–10. John had one word for the victory, well, three words: "Awesome," he said. "Just awesome."

Even more awesome was Denver's 24–21 win over the Pittsburgh Steelers in the AFC Championship game the next week. Terrell ran all over the Steelers, gaining 139 yards on 26 carries. The Broncos were going to the Super Bowl! There, the powerful Green Bay Packers were waiting for them.

UNDERDOG DENVER

No one gave the Broncos much of a chance against Green Bay. The Packers were the defending Super Bowl champs. Not to mention that Denver was 0–4 in Super Bowls, including 0–3 with John. The experts predicted Green Bay would win big.

At first, it looked as if that might happen. The Packers scored on their first possession and led, 7–0. But the Broncos fought back. Near the end of the third quarter, the score was tied, 17–17. Denver faced a crucial third-down play.

The Broncos had the ball on Green Bay's 12-yard line. A first down was six yards away. John dropped back to pass, but his receivers were covered. He decided to run for the first down. Instead of playing it safe and sliding in front of the defender or running out-of-bounds, he sprinted into the open field. John spun around in mid-air after a collision with Packer safety LeRoy Butler. When he landed, he had gained eight yards and the first down. It was a *huge* play.

"When I saw him do that and then get up pumping his fist, I said, 'It's on,'" said Shannon Sharpe. "That's when I was sure we were going to win."

Shannon was right about that. Denver beat Green Bay,

31–24. The Broncos had won their first Super Bowl! Terrell had missed the entire second quarter with a bad headache called a migraine. But he ended the game with 157 rushing yards and three touchdowns. Terrell was named the Most Valuable Player (MVP).

LET'S WIN TWO!

T he 1998 Broncos were even better than the 1997 team. They were almost perfect. The 1972 Miami Dolphins are the only team to go undefeated for an entire season *(see box on page 11)*. But the 1998 Broncos came close. They won 13 straight games before losing on a last-minute play to the New York Giants. They finished the regular season with a 14–2 record.

The key to Denver's success was its stability. All but three starting players from the previous season were back. They worked well together. This stability was especially helpful to the defense. Denver had given up big plays on defense in past seasons. In 1998, it was stopping opponents cold.

Denver's talent pool was deeper than ever. When John had hamstring and back problems, backup quarterback Bubby Brister stepped in and saved the day. The Broncos' special teams also contributed to the team's success. Kicker Jason Elam was magnificent. He made 23 of 27 field-goal attempts and kicked a 63-yard field goal that tied the NFL record!

Of course, the offense was as amazing as ever. Terrell rushed for 2,008 yards on 392 carries and led the league in rushing yards and scoring. Wide receiver Ed McCaffrey had his best season with 10 touchdowns and 1,053 receiving yards. The offense averaged 31.3 points per game.

The loss to the Giants late in the regular season may have been good for the Broncos. When the team was undefeated, the players were under a lot of pressure. It was a relief when their 13-game streak ended. "It was wearing me down," said defensive tackle Keith Traylor. "Everywhere I went, people would ask, 'You guys going undefeated?' And I always told them, 'I don't know. I just want to win the Super Bowl.'"

That was the ultimate prize: a *second* Super Bowl triumph. The Broncos had little trouble getting it. They clobbered the Miami Dolphins with a 38–3 win in the divisional playoff. They defeated the New York Jets, 23–10, in the AFC Championship Game. In the Super Bowl, they destroyed the Atlanta Falcons, 34–19.

The victory was a total team effort. Terrell ran for 102 yards on 25 carries. John played well. He threw for 336 yards and a touchdown. He was named the game's MVP. The 38-year-old quarterback was thrilled. No one could question his ability to win The Big One anymore. He could retire in peace. John and his talented team put those questions to rest.

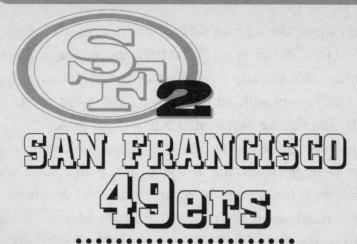

SAN FRANCISCO
49ers

∙ ∙

Outstanding play and five Super Bowl wins made this team an NFL powerhouse

When you talk about football and greatness, you have to start with the San Francisco 49ers. No NFL team has matched the run the 49ers had from 1982 through 1995. They played in the Super Bowl five times (1982, 1985, 1989, 1990, 1995) in 14 seasons and won all five games! Going five-for-five is an NFL record.

The key to San Francisco's success was obvious: talented players and talented head coaches. During those years, the team had not one, but two of the best quarterbacks in the history of the NFL — Joe Montana and Steve Young. Catching Joe and Steve's passes were All-Pros Dwight Clark, John Taylor, and Jerry Rice. Jerry is the best wide receiver of all time. He has caught more passes and scored more touchdowns than any player in NFL history. Two star running backs who helped lead the charge were Roger Craig (1983-90) and Ricky Watters (1991-94).

But that was just on offense! The 49ers had a top-notch defense that included defensive lineman Charles Haley, cornerback Deion Sanders, and safeties Merton Hanks and Ronnie Lott. Charles was the first NFL player to play in and win five Super Bowls (two with the 49ers and three with Dallas). Deion was the NFL Defensive Player of the Year in 1994. Ronnie and Merton snatched many interceptions.

The 49ers were guided through those seasons by coaches Bill Walsh (1979-88) and George Seifert (1989-96), two of the best ever. Except for the 1983 season, when there was a strike, San Francisco won at least 10 games every season between 1981 and 1994. It had the best record in the National Football Conference (NFC) seven times!

JOE THE PRO

When Coach Walsh took over as head coach, in 1979, the 49ers did not look like a great team — or like they would ever be one. The club had a dismal 2–14 record the season before Coach Walsh arrived. They had the same sad result (2–14) in his first season.

The one good thing about having such a horrible record

is that you get to go first in the NFL draft of players coming out of college. Coach Walsh took advantage of this and picked some great talent. In the 1979 NFL draft, the 49ers selected quarterback Joe Montana and receiver Dwight Clark. Two years later, they drafted safety Ronnie Lott. These three players became the core of the team that won San Francisco its first Super Bowl, in 1982.

Ronnie became the heart and soul of the defense. He was one of football's most fearsome hitters at the safety position. He helped the 49er defense snatch 27 interceptions in his first season — the most by a 49er defense in

THE CATCH

The Dallas Cowboys were ahead of the 49ers, 27–21, with 58 seconds left to play in the NFC Championship Game, in 1982. The 49ers were six yards from the end zone. Joe Montana couldn't see receiver Dwight Clark, but he knew that Dwight was supposed to be cutting across the back of the end zone.

Joe fired an off-balance pass seconds before he was tackled. The ball went over Dwight's head, but he leaped high into the air and caught the ball — the winning touchdown! The great play that became known as "The Catch" sent the 49ers to their first Super Bowl.

30 years! Dwight averaged 56 catches per season from 1979 through 1987. He's most famous, though, for making "The Catch" *(see box on page 18)* that beat the Dallas Cowboys in the 1982 NFC Championship game.

And then there was Joe. Joe had had a stellar college career at the University of Notre Dame. But as an NFL rookie, in 1979, he threw only 23 passes all season! In 1980, he began the season on the bench but, eventually, won the starting job. The 49ers improved their season record to 6–10.

Joe had many great qualities. He had an accurate arm. He had excellent field vision. He seemed to know where all the players on the field were and what each player was doing at any given time. Joe could also see what the other team's defense was doing and figure out how to beat it.

But Joe's greatest quality was his leadership. He didn't panic when a play didn't work. He was tough and he never gave up. As an example, in his first year as a starter, Joe and the 49ers trailed the New Orleans Saints 35–7 at half-time. Joe led the 49ers back to win the game, 38–35, in overtime! Joe became famous for his last-minute come-backs. The bigger the game, the better Joe played.

In the Super Bowl — the biggest game of all — Joe threw 122 passes and no interceptions in his four appearances! He set Super Bowl records for most career touchdowns (11), most career yards gained (1,142), and most career completions (83). He completed 68 percent of his passes. No wonder he was named Super Bowl MVP three times!

In the 1989 Super Bowl, Joe led the 49ers 92 yards to a game-winning touchdown in the closing minutes to beat the Cincinnati Bengals, 20–16. He finished the game with a Super Bowl-record 357 passing yards as the 49ers won their third championship.

In 1990, the 49ers played the Denver Broncos. It was the 33-year-old quarterback's last Super Bowl. He completed 22 of 29 passes for 297 yards and five touchdowns! The 49ers destroyed Denver, 55–10, and Joe became the only player to be named Most Valuable Player in three Super Bowls.

RUN, CATCH, WIN!

Even after the 49ers became one of the best teams in the NFL, they still continued to choose well in the NFL draft. In 1983, they selected running back Roger Craig from Nebraska. Two years later, they picked up wide receiver Jerry Rice from Mississippi Valley State.

Roger was football's ultimate double threat. He was tough and powerful, but he also caught the ball as well as any other running back ever to play in the NFL. For opponents, that spelled double trouble! The combination enabled Roger to do something no one had ever done: In 1985, he became the first running back to gain more than

THE STEEL CURTAIN

Does winning four Super Bowls seem like a big deal? Maybe not, since San Francisco and Dallas have both won five. But four was fantastic in 1980 when the Pittsburgh Steelers became the first team to do it. They won in 1975, 1976, 1979, and 1980.

Hall of Famer Terry Bradshaw quarterbacked a well-balanced offense that included running back Franco Harris and Pro Bowl wide receivers Lynn Swann and John Stallworth. Terry won two Super Bowl MVP awards, and Franco rushed for nearly 12,000 yards in his 12 years as a Steeler. Lynn was named Super Bowl MVP during the Steelers second championship season, and John broke team records for career receptions and receiving yards.

Pittsburgh's offense was good, but the team was known for its tough defense. The Steeler defense was nicknamed the Steel Curtain. (The nickname came from "Iron Curtain," the name used to describe the heavily defended former Communist countries of Eastern Europe.) The Steel Curtain stars included four Hall of Famers: linebackers Jack Lambert and Jack Ham, defensive lineman "Mean" Joe Greene, and cornerback Mel Blount.

"We could not and would not accept a loss," Terry said. "We laughed and giggled and had fun playing, but we had fangs and the blood and the slobber, too. We wanted it."

1,000 rushing yards and 1,000 receiving yards in the same season! In 1990, Roger set the record for the most career passes caught in Super Bowl games (20).

Roger's record was broken in the 1995 Super Bowl — by teammate Jerry Rice. Jerry caught 28 passes in three Super Bowls! Jerry broke a lot of other records, too. He had played at a small college, Mississippi Valley State. He had not played against the best college players. But it didn't take Jerry long to prove that he could keep up with them just fine! In only his second season, he led the league in touchdown receptions (15) and receiving yards (1,570).

Jerry went on to set the all-time NFL career records for most receptions, yardage, and touchdowns. And, like Joe Montana, Jerry played better the more important the game was. In January 1989, he caught 11 balls for 215 yards in the Super Bowl and was named the game's MVP. Jerry also set career Super Bowl records for touchdowns (7), receptions (28), and yards gained (512).

Jerry and fellow receiver John Taylor were the perfect players for what became known as the "West Coast offense." This was an offensive system created by Coach Walsh in the early 1970's. It depended on short passes that receivers could turn into big gains. Jerry and John caught short passes, called "slants," over the middle of the field. Then they used their great speed to outrun defenders. With all that talent and a smart system, San Francisco was almost unstoppable from 1981 to 1988.

Coach Seifert *[SEE-fert]* took over the team in 1989. He kept Coach Walsh's system — and the 49ers kept winning.

YOUNG TALENT

·······························

A s the San Francisco stars of the 1980's grew older, the 49ers had to find talented young players to replace them. They already had a terrific quarterback waiting in the wings: Steve Young. Steve's first four seasons as a pro had been frustrating. He played two seasons in the United States Football League, but the league folded in 1985. Then Steve joined the Tampa Bay Buccaneers. The Bucs had a horrible 4–28 record during Steve's two seasons with them, and many people blamed Steve.

But the 49ers didn't blame Steve. In 1987, they traded two draft picks for him. They wanted Steve to take over for Joe, eventually. Steve sat on the bench for four seasons and learned the offense, until 1991, when Joe hurt his elbow.

In his first full season (1991), Steve was the NFL's highest-rated quarterback. The NFL rates its passers using a formula that measures completion percentage, yards, touchdowns, and interceptions. He had the highest rating five more times: in 1992, 1993, 1994, 1996, and 1997.

But Steve's success as a passer was not enough to get the

49ers back to the Super Bowl in the first three seasons he started as quarterback. Many people wondered if Steve had the leadership qualities needed to win a championship.

By the start of the 1994 season, San Francisco had acquired some new talent. Running back Ricky Watters, linebacker Ken Norton, Junior, and flashy cornerback Deion Sanders joined a defense that already included Merton Hanks and Eric Davis. If Steve was ever going to win the NFL championship, 1994 was the season.

RECORD MAKERS

Steve's 1994 regular season was his best yet. He finished the season with 3,969 yards and 35 touchdowns. But Steve wasn't the only 49er who played well that season. Jerry was catching everything in sight. Deion returned three interceptions for touchdowns and was named the NFL's Defensive Player of the Year.

The 49ers had finished the regular season 13–3. But could they win the 1995 Super Bowl? Not a problem! San Francisco trounced the San Diego Chargers, 49–26. Steve threw a Super Bowl record six touchdowns and was named MVP. He had finally filled Joe's shoes!

The "drive for five" had been a success. The 49ers became the first NFL team to win five Super Bowl titles. And they had done it in just 14 seasons.

3

THE DALLAS COWBOYS

A trio of stars sparked Dallas to three Super Bowl victories in four years

Is there something special about the number 3? Maybe for the Dallas Cowboys, there is. In 1996, the Dallas Cowboys became the first team to win three Super Bowls in four years. They did it in large part because of three great players. Most teams that win a Super Bowl have either a great quarterback, a great running back, or a great wide receiver. Sometimes they have two of those. The Cowboys of the 1990's had all three!

But the team's rise to glory didn't start with great players. It actually began with a new owner and a new coach.

Jerry Jones bought the Cowboys in 1989. Dallas *had* been one of the most successful and popular teams in NFL history.

In the 1970's, they played in five of 10 Super Bowls! They won two of them, in 1972 and 1978. The Cowboys became so popular around the country that they were called "America's Team."

By 1989, however, "America's Team" was falling apart. The Cowboys' record in 1988 was a dismal 3–13. Mr. Jones knew that changes had to be made. He didn't hesitate.

The first thing Mr. Jones did was hire Jimmy Johnson to be the new head coach. Coach Johnson had been very successful as a college football coach. He had won a national championship at the University of Miami. Still, success with a college team doesn't always mean success in the pros. But Jimmy Johnson loved a challenge.

Coach Johnson remade the team roster completely. He wanted to build a young, fast team that had players with plenty of self-confidence. He once put it this way: "The people I want around me, well, the bigger the game, the more they shine."

The Cowboys did not shine in Coach Johnson's first season. They won only one game and lost 15! But they were building for the future. Quarterback Troy Aikman was a rookie. He gained lots of experience. Second-year receiver Michael Irvin was injured in 1989 but was excited about playing for Coach Johnson, who had been his coach in college. After the season, the Cowboys chose running back

Emmitt Smith in the first round of the NFL draft. These three players soon became the team's offensive leaders.

TALENTED TRIO

Troy was the perfect quarterback to lead the Cowboys. Sure, he was young and inexperienced, but he was Coach Johnson's type of player because he hated to lose. Through hard work, Troy made himself into one of the league's best quarterbacks. He became known for the pinpoint accuracy of his throws.

Troy was a "pocket passer." He didn't do a lot of running around but preferred to stay right behind his offensive linemen. As a result, he took a lot of hits from the opposing defenders. But Troy was tough. He did whatever it took to complete a pass — even if he paid for it by being tackled.

Best of all, Troy was able to stay calm and take charge in pressure situations. That made him the perfect fit for Coach Johnson's aggressive style of football. While many coaches are more concerned with protecting the ball and not taking a lot of chances, Coach Johnson liked to take risks.

"That's been our style ever since I've been here," Troy said once. "Always go for it, always attack, no matter what the score is."

Having Michael Irvin as their wide receiver made it easy for the Cowboys to attack. Michael's nickname was "The

Playmaker," and his statistics tell you why. From 1991 to 1995, Michael averaged 90 catches for 1,419 yards and eight touchdowns per season. Michael could do it all. He was great at streaking downfield and catching the long pass, but he could also grab short passes in a lot of traffic. At 6' 2'', Michael was a big, physical receiver who used his body to out-muscle defensive players.

Michael was also Dallas's emotional leader. If he didn't think a teammate was trying hard enough, he let the player know about it. When things weren't going well for the team, he was the first one to try to get his teammates pumped up to turn those things around.

Troy and Michael were key to the team's improvement, but the most important Cowboy was Emmitt Smith. Whenever Dallas needed some yards that were tough to get, Emmitt got them. Whenever they needed to protect a lead by grinding out first downs with their running game, Emmitt got them. He was unstoppable.

What made Emmitt so great was his combination of speed and power. He was fast enough to go around defenders and pull away for long gains, and he was strong enough to go *through* defenses. In his first six seasons, Emmitt ran for 8,956 yards and 96 touchdowns. He led the league in rushing four times in those years. In 1996, he set the record for most career rushing touchdowns in the Super Bowl. ⟹

THE FIRST DALLAS DYNASTY

How many coaches did the Cowboys have before Jimmy Johnson came in 1989? Just one. But what a coach! His name was Tom Landry. He coached the team to a 270-178-6 record over 29 seasons, from 1960 to 1988. During the time he was the coach, Dallas:

★ set an NFL record for winning seasons with 20 in a row!
★ earned 18 playoff appearances and 13 divisional titles
★ played in five Super Bowls
★ won two of them!

How did Coach Landry do it? First of all, he had the players. Those 1970's teams were stocked with talent on both offense and defense. Quarterback Roger Staubach, running back Tony Dorsett, and wide receivers Drew Pearson and "Bullet" Bob Hayes led the attack. On defense, linemen Harvey Martin, Randy White, and Ed "Too Tall" Jones were among the best to play the game.

Second, Coach Landry set a tone that the players took up. They didn't brag about their success; they let their play speak for itself. It spoke loudly!

With Troy, Michael, and Emmitt on board, Dallas had all the pieces in place for a Super Bowl run. In the 1992 season, they made that run. Emmitt ran for 1,713 yards and scored 18 touchdowns. Dallas finished the regular season with a 13–3 record.

CHAMPIONS!

In the NFC Championship Game, the Cowboys went into San Francisco and shocked the 49ers, 30–20! Nobody expected Dallas to make it to the Super Bowl so quickly. The players were still young. They didn't have the experience. But the offense was powerful. Troy, Michael, and Emmitt were champions — and they proved it in the Super Bowl.

The Cowboys faced the Buffalo Bills in the January 1993 game. The Bills were an experienced team. They were playing in their third straight Super Bowl.

No matter. Emmitt ran for 108 yards, and Michael caught two touchdown passes. Troy completed 22 of 30 passes for 273 yards and four touchdowns. Dallas clobbered Buffalo, 52–17. Troy, who was 26 years old, was named Super Bowl MVP. In his three playoff games that season, Troy had thrown for eight touchdowns and no interceptions!

Dallas's defense was even better than its offense. Coach Johnson had built his defense around speed instead of size.

He wanted smaller players who could react and move quickly to the action. Ken Norton, Junior, Leon Lett, James Washington, Charles Haley, and the other Dallas defenders did just that, and it made them the best defense in the league.

In the Super Bowl, the Dallas defenders were terrific. They forced Buffalo into a Super Bowl-record nine turnovers. They ran two of those turnovers in for touchdowns. Three turnovers set up other Dallas touchdowns. Afterward, even Troy was amazed at what the defense had done. "I've never seen a defensive performance like that in my entire life," Troy told Coach Johnson. "Just awesome."

REPEAT!

The next season, Dallas dominated the NFL again. In 1993-94, Emmitt led the league in rushing and was named the league's MVP. The Cowboys again met the 49ers in the NFC Championship Game. Coach Johnson was as confident as ever, and he wanted his players to be confident, as well. What did he do? He called a radio show before the big game and guaranteed a victory!

"We will win the game," Coach Johnson said. "You can put it in three-inch headlines." He was right! The Cowboys scored four touchdowns in the first half on their way to a 38–21 win. They were also on their way back to the Super Bowl for a rematch with Buffalo.

In the title game, the Bills took a 13–6 lead into halftime. But then, on the third (yes, *third*) play of the second half, the Dallas defense came alive. Leon Lett hit Buffalo running back Thurman Thomas and caused a fumble. James Washington scooped up the ball and ran it back 46 yards for a touchdown!

Buffalo did not score again. James, who had forced a fumble himself in the first half, caught an interception late in the game to seal the 30–13 Dallas victory. On offense, Troy completed 19 of 27 passes, and Emmitt rushed 30 times for 132 yards and two touchdowns. He was named MVP. "I wish there were some way they could have given co-awards," Emmitt said of his MVP trophy, "so that James Washington could have gotten something."

James — and all the other Cowboys — did get something: another Super Bowl win! But little did they know that the captain of their ship, Jimmy Johnson, was preparing to set sail elsewhere.

MOVIN' ON

Although Dallas had won two straight Super Bowls, not all was well within the organization. The owner and the coach had not been getting along. After the second Super Bowl victory, Coach Johnson decided to leave the team. Mr. Jones replaced him with former University of Oklahoma coach Barry Switzer.

Several players, including Michael and Troy, were very upset about the change. But the Cowboys went 12–4 under Coach Switzer in 1994 and made it to the NFC Championship Game before losing to San Francisco.

Cornerback Deion Sanders joined the team for the 1995 season. Deion was an exciting player who electrified the defense with his ability to make big plays. Emmitt had another awesome season, in 1995, setting an NFL record with 25 touchdowns. The Cowboys cruised to a 12–4 regular-season mark and through the playoffs. After a year away, "America's Team" was back in the Super Bowl!

The Cowboys faced the Pittsburgh Steelers this time. The Cowboys jumped to a 10–0 lead in the game. In the third quarter, they were clinging to a 13–7 lead and Pittsburgh had the ball. Suddenly, a little-known cornerback named Larry Brown took over the game! Larry was thought to be a weak link in the Dallas defense.

But two days before the Super Bowl, Larry had predicted he would get two interceptions. And he did! Larry's two interceptions set up rushing touchdowns by Emmitt. Dallas won 27–17, and Larry was voted MVP.

The Cowboys had become only the second NFL team to win five Super Bowl championships. They were the first to win three Super Bowls in four years. For Dallas, the number three was just one of several lucky numbers.

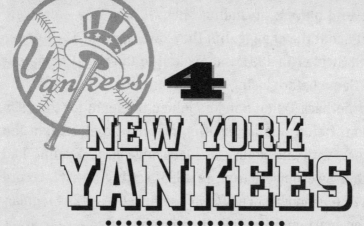

4
NEW YORK YANKEES

• •

When they won the 1998 World Series, they did it in record fashion

The Yankees are a team that people have strong feelings about. Many fans love them. Other people hate them. But even the people who hate them are impressed by what they have done over the years. In pro sports, only the Montreal Canadiens hockey team *(see page 79)* has won as many championships as the Yankees. Entering the 1998 season, the Yankees had won an amazing 23 World Series. But the most amazing was yet to come.

In 1998, the Yankees won the team's 24th World Series — with a four-game sweep of the San Diego Padres, no less. They also won more games than any other baseball team ever! Counting the regular season, playoffs, and World

Series, the 1998 Yankees won an incredible 125 games and lost only 50. These Yankees might have been more than the best team in baseball, they might have been the best team in baseball history! Even Yankee-haters were impressed.

A BOLD PREDICTION

he Yankees' run for the 1998 title actually began in 1997. New York had just lost to the Cleveland Indians in the divisional playoff series. Even as disappointed players still sat in the locker room after the final game, team owner George Steinbrenner had a message for the baseball world: "We'll win it all next year. Mark that down."

Mr. Steinbrenner had reason for his optimism. The Yankees had outstanding talent, and they knew how to win. Just a year earlier, in 1996, they had won the World Series. Many of the key players from that team were still playing for the Yanks. Centerfielder Bernie Williams, rightfielder Paul O'Neill, and shortstop Derek Jeter led a powerful lineup. Andy Pettitte and David Cone led a talented pitching staff. All New York needed was a little fine-tuning to become serious contenders again in 1998.

During the off-season, the Yankees took care of that fine-tuning. First, they picked up designated hitter Chili Davis. Then they traded for second baseman Chuck Knoblauch and third baseman Scott Brosius to shore up their infield.

Finally, they went searching for another pitcher. They came up with Cuban star Orlando "El Duque *[DOO-kay]*" Hernandez. The Yankees were ready for their run at greatness.

BETTER AND BETTER

As spring training began, New York looked good. The Yankees were solid at every single position and had one of the best pitching staffs in the game. When the season began, New York lost its first three games. The team then recovered to win 17 of its next 20 games and finished the month of April with a 17–6 record.

The Yankees continued their dominance in May, winning another 20 games. Best of all, the team had found another star. Left-handed pitcher David Wells had had a 106–80 record over 11 seasons in the majors. On May 17, he threw a perfect game against the Minnesota Twins. What was so perfect about it? David didn't give up a hit or a walk. Not one Twin batter got on base. The Yankees won, 4–0. "Right now, I'm the happiest man on Earth," David said after his masterpiece.

David ended up with a strong 18–4 record for the season. Andy, David Cone, and El Duque pitched well, too. In April, Andy had a streak in which he allowed only three earned runs in 27 ⅓ innings. David Cone's earned run average for the month of July was an astonishing 0.69, the lowest in baseball. El Duque made his major league debut on June 3 against the Tampa Bay Devil Rays after having nine starts in the minors. He allowed only one run and five hits in a 7–1 Yankee victory. He got even better as the season went on and finished with a 12–4 record.

As if the starting pitching weren't strong enough, the Yankees also had the American League's top relief pitcher in Mariano Rivera. Mariano was New York's "closer," which means he was usually brought in late in the game to help the team hold onto a lead. With Mariano in the game, the Yankees knew their lead was safe.

THE PRIDE OF THE YANKEES

While the Yankee pitchers were shutting down the opposition, New York's hitters were pounding the ball. They did not have any super-sluggers, but the Yanks had a lineup full of solid hitters. The team finished with 207 home runs, which put them fourth in the A.L., yet not one player hit more than 30. Instead, they became one of only two teams in baseball history to have 10 players hit 10 or more homers each.

As the season continued, it seemed a new hero would emerge each month. In June, Paul hit .333 with six home runs and four stolen bases. In July, Derek hit .336 with four homers and five doubles. The Yankees ran their won-lost mark to 76–27. In August, Bernie drove in 28 runs. He went on to win the American League batting title with a .339 average. He smacked 26 home runs on the season.

Then in September, rookie Shane Spencer came out of nowhere and hit an eye-opening .421, with eight home runs and 21 RBIs, in only 38 at bats. Shane blasted three grand slams in 10 days — as many as Yankee manager Joe Torre had hit in his entire 18-season playing career!

The Yankees finished the regular season with a record of 114–48. That was the most wins ever by an American League team. (Only the National League's 1906 Chicago Cubs, with 116 wins, have more.) Many experts began to call New York the best team of all-time.

Even the Yankees started to wonder.

"Anytime you can start talking about the best whatever in baseball, that's special," said Joe Torre. "This game has been around a long time, and anytime you accomplish something historic, you have to feel proud."

If there was one word that summed up the 1998 Yankees, it was just that: *pride*. The team had talent, for sure, but it also worked harder and played better together than anyone else. A loss was never acceptable. "We've said all along that we're not satisfied to just play pretty well," Scott said. "There's a desire in all of us to win every game."

Scott was the perfect example of that desire. In 1997, he

MURDERERS' ROW

As good as the 1998 Yankees were, they may not have been the best Yankee team ever — at least when it comes to hitting. The 1927 Yankees had the most devastating group of sluggers baseball has ever seen. They became known as Murderers' Row because so many team members could absolutely kill the ball.

At the heart of that legendary lineup were two of the best players of all time: Babe Ruth and Lou Gehrig. In 1927, Babe not only hit .356 and drove in 164 runs, but he also slammed 60 home runs. That set a single-season record that stood for 34 years! But Babe wasn't even named the American League's Most Valuable Player! That honor went to Lou. Lou hit .373, with 175 RBIs and 47 home runs.

New York had a 110–44 regular-season record in 1927 and was confident going into the World Series against the Pittsburgh Pirates. (There were no playoffs at the time.) How confident were they? Before the Series, second baseman Tony Lazzeri said, "If we don't beat these bums four in a row, you can shoot me."

No one had to shoot Tony: The Yankees swept the Pirates in four games, and the 1927 Yankees went down in history as one of the Top Teams Ever in sports.

played third base for the Oakland A's and hit a measly .203. But the Yankees traded for him anyway. Scott was the surprise player of 1998. He hit .300, with 19 homers and 98 RBIs. He also played great defense and became a team leader. Scott's unexpected success helped turn New York into a powerhouse.

The Yankees totally dominated the regular season, winning more than 70 percent of their games. Even better, they led the majors in runs scored while allowing the fewest amount of runs to score *against* them in their league. But would their success carry over into the playoffs? Winning 114 games wouldn't mean anything unless New York brought home a World Series championship.

ON A ROLL

Things started off smoothly. The Yankees swept the Texas Rangers in three games in the divisional playoffs. But the American League Championship Series was not so easy. New York faced the Cleveland Indians, who had eliminated New York the season before. The Indians were good, so good, in fact, that they won two of the first three games of the series! If the Yankees lost Game 4, they would be one game away from elimination.

Manager Torre sent El Duque to the mound for Game 4. When the Yanks came to bat, Paul started the game off with a first-inning home run. That was a good sign. El Duque pitched seven innings of shutout ball. Relievers Mike Stanton and Mariano Rivera shut down the Indians the rest of the way and New York won, 4–0.

After that game, the Yankees never looked back. They won the next two games and were on their way to the World Series.

A RECORD RUN

Facing New York in the Series were the San Diego Padres. In Game 1, San Diego took a surprising 5–2 lead into the seventh inning. But the Yankees were too good a team to let this throw them. New York erupted for seven runs in the bottom of the seventh inning. Any momentum the Padres thought they might have was gone. The Yankees won the opener, 9–6, and added a 9–3 demolition of the Padres in Game 2.

The Yankees staged another dramatic comeback in Game 3 after they once again found themselves down by three runs entering the seventh inning. This time, one player led the rally as Scott smacked home runs in both the seventh and eighth innings. Scott became only the eighth player in World Series history to hit homers in back-to-back innings.

"This is the type of thing you dream about as a kid," Scott

said afterward. "And you never know if you're going to get the opportunity to do it."

The Yankees won Game 3 by a score of 5–4, and then closed out the series with a 3–0 shutout in Game 4. The sweep of the National League champion Padres gave New York a record of 125 wins and 50 losses. No team in baseball history had ever won so many games.

TEAM CHEMISTRY

The Yankee achievement was one of the great team efforts of all time. Everyone had helped contribute to this World Series triumph.

Scott, the third baseman nobody wanted a year earlier, was named World Series MVP for his .471 batting and six RBIs. "When I think of this team, you know what's going to come to mind? Scotty Brosius," Joe Torre said. "His personality was a big part of this club."

By getting contributions from every member of the team, New York had proven that hard work and team chemistry paid off. And no one could argue with the results.

"This has to go down as one of the best teams of all time," Derek said after the Yankees had been crowned World Champions. "I can't see anybody dominating the league the way we did. I mean, we were 125 and 50? That's ridiculous."

Yankee fans and haters alike would agree.

THE CINCINNATI REDS

• • • • • • • • • • • • • • •

Loaded with talent, the Reds rolled to two straight World Series wins

When is a baseball team not a team? When it's a Big Red Machine. The Big Red Machine was the nickname for the Cincinnati Reds of the mid-1970's. Why? Because they got into gear and dominated the National League (N.L.) with hitting, speed, and defense. They rolled to two straight World Series titles as if they were some kind of unstoppable machine.

In the early '70's, the Reds were a good team but it looked as if they might never win the World Series. Three times they won the N.L. West division title (in 1970, 1972, 1973). In 1970 and '72, they advanced to the World Series and lost. In 1974, they finished second in the N.L. West.

When the 1975 season began, the Reds didn't look good. On May 3, 1975, they had a 12–12 record and were three games behind the division-leading Los Angeles Dodgers. Then Reds manager Sparky Anderson did something that turned the team around: He moved Pete Rose from the outfield to third base. Pete was one of Cincinnati's best players and he was a good outfielder. But moving him to third base opened up room for another great player, George Foster, to play leftfield. George had been playing only part-time until then.

George was a powerful hitter, and with him in the line-up, the Reds passed the Dodgers and began winning at a record pace. By the All-Star break, in July, the Reds had a 61–29 record. During one 50-game stretch, they went 41–9. When the regular season ended, they had 108 wins. That was the most by a National League team in 66 years! The Reds won the division by *20 games* over the Dodgers.

BATS ALIVE!

How did they do it? They started with lots of out-standing hitting. First baseman Tony Perez slugged his way to a .282 batting average, with 20 home runs and 109 runs batted in (RBIs). Catcher Johnny Bench hit 28 home runs and drove in 110 runs. Pete hit .317 and scored 112 runs. (Pete would go on to set the record for most hits in a career with 4,256, that's how good a hitter he was!) Second baseman Joe Morgan stole 67 bases and had a team-record 132 walks. He also hit .327, with 17 home runs and 94 RBIs. He was named the N.L. 1975 MVP.

In all, the Reds hit a combined .271 with 124 homers. They led the league with 840 runs scored. "Every time we walked onto the field, everybody knew the Reds were going to score a lot of runs," Tony said. "We could be eight runs down in the seventh inning and still believe we were going to win."

ARMS, HANDS, AND FEET

But hitting wasn't the only thing the Reds did well. They could also run! The team led the league with 168 stolen bases. Joe, shortstop Dave Concepcion, and rightfielder Ken Griffey (who is the father of Seattle Mariner superstar Ken Griffey, Junior) were all terrific base stealers.

On top of that, the Reds had the best defense in the league. Johnny Bench was a great catcher, perhaps the greatest ever. He, Joe, Dave, and centerfielder Cesar *[SAY-zar]* Geronimo all won Gold Gloves for being the best defensive players at their positions. That meant that Cincinnati had the best defensive players up the middle of the field — the most important place to be strong.

As if that were not enough, Cincinnati had good

pitching, too! There were no superstar pitchers on the team, but there was a group of solid starters and outstanding relievers. Three of the starters — Jack Billingham, Gary Nolan, and Don Gullett — each won 15 games in 1975. Four relievers had earned run averages (ERAs) under 3.00. They were Clay Carroll (2.63 ERA), Pedro Borbon (2.95), Will McEnaney (2.47), and Rawley Eastwick (2.60). Rawley also led the league with 22 saves.

Put together all that hitting, power, speed, defense, and pitching, and the Reds were the best team in baseball. And they knew it. "What made it so much fun back then," said Rawley, "is that when you came to the ballpark, you knew you were going to win that day."

CHAMPS AT LAST!

The Reds met the Boston Red Sox in the 1975 World Series. Cincinnati led three games to two and Game 6 was one of the most dramatic games ever. The Reds took a 6–3 lead into the bottom of the eighth inning and was just six outs away from winning the championship.

Then Boston pinch hitter Bernie Carbo hit a three-run home run to tie the score! The game went into extra innings and finally ended in the bottom of the 12th. Red Sox catcher Carlton Fisk hit a huge blast to leftfield. He started down the base path, waving at the ball as though he

MEANWHILE, IN THE AMERICAN LEAGUE . . .

While the Reds were dominating the National League in the 1970's, another terrific team ruled over the American League. The Oakland Athletics, or the A's, as they are called, won five straight A.L. West division titles, from 1971 through 1975. And they won three straight World Series crowns in 1972, '73, and '74.

The A's moved to Oakland, California, from Kansas City, Missouri, in 1968. As soon as they arrived, they started to win! In 1968, they had their first winning season in 16 years. After second-place finishes in 1969 and 1970, the A's began their impressive run of titles. They were sparked by rightfielder Reggie Jackson, who led the A.L. in home runs four times in his career. Reggie played his best in the playoffs. In the 1973 World Series, he drove in six runs and hit .310 to win MVP honors as the A's beat the New York Mets in seven games.

But Oakland's great strength was its pitching. In 1973, Vida Blue, Catfish Hunter, and Ken Holtzman each won 20 games. Rollie Fingers was baseball's best relief pitcher. In the 1974 World Series, he saved two games and won another during Oakland's 4–1 victory over the Dodgers. In the early 1970's, major league baseball really got straight "A's!"

could will it to stay fair. The ball hit the foul pole. It was a home run! Boston won the game, 7–6, and tied the series at three games apiece!

Had Cincinnati blown its best chance to win the World Series? It looked like it when Boston took an early 3–0 lead in Game 7. But the Reds tied the score in the seventh inning. Then, with two outs in the ninth inning, Joe Morgan hit the ball off the very end of his bat. *Single!* The hit drove in a run to give Cincinnati a 4–3 win — and their first world championship in 35 years!

"We are the best team in baseball," manager Sparky Anderson said afterward.

LEAGUE LEADERS

No one could argue: The 1975 Reds were the best. Believe it or not, though, they were as good, or better, in 1976! The Big Red Machine won 102 regular-season games and dominated the National League in every way possible that year.

Once again, the Reds were the best-hitting team in baseball. Five players finished the season with batting averages above .300. Ken Griffey finished second in the National League with a .336 average. Pete (.323) finished fourth, and Joe (.320) finished fifth. Joe also had 27 home runs and 111 RBIs, and collected his second straight MVP award.

Cesar hit .307, and George Foster hit .306 with 29 home runs and a league-best 121 RBIs.

As a team, the Reds hitters led the N.L. in nine categories: hits, doubles, triples, home runs, walks, batting average, on-base percentage, slugging percentage, and runs scored. They continued to display great speed, defense, and pitching, as well, leading the league in stolen bases, fielding percentage, and saves.

ROYAL REDS

Because they were so good, the Reds were treated by fans as baseball royalty. "Everywhere we went, in every town, people started talking before our plane touched down: 'Here comes the Big Red Machine!' " said Tony. "The Big Red Machine. Oh, I loved that name. We all did. We all knew what it meant."

What it meant was that Cincinnati had so much talent that they were simply overpowering. "If there ever was a time when another team did approach our level of play," said George, "we would shift into an even higher gear, just like a machine."

The Reds never felt pressure or lost their confidence. If they got into trouble, it seemed as if they could just flick a switch and play better. "That team was as good as it wanted to be," Manager Sparky Anderson said. "If it wanted to be perfect on a given day, it was. . . . I've always preached,

'You can't turn it on and off.' Well, that team could."

The regular season was just a tune-up for the real show — the playoffs. In the National League Championship Series, Cincinnati faced a strong Philadelphia Phillies team. The Phillies had won 101 regular-season games, just one fewer than the Reds. No matter. Behind Pete's .429 average, Cincinnati swept the Phillies in three straight games.

A DATE WITH HISTORY

Next up was another trip to the World Series, against the New York Yankees. Joe made a statement by hitting a home run in the first inning of Game 1. The Yankees never recovered. The Reds swept New York in four games to win their second straight World Series crown.

Cincinnati had not been playing just against the Yankees. They had been playing against history. With the World Series victory, the Big Red Machine became the first N.L. team in *54 years* to repeat as world champions. They also became the first team, after the introduction of the league championship series in 1969, to go undefeated in the post-season. (Through 1998, no team had matched that feat!)

"We weren't out to prove that we were one of the greatest teams of all time," George said later. "But when we were at our best, no one could approach us."

6

THE CHICAGO BULLS

• • • • • • • • • • • • • • • • • • •

Michael Jordan and company powered the Bulls to six titles in eight years

When people think of the Chicago Bulls' championship years, they tend to think about one player: Michael Jordan. There is a good reason for that. Michael is the best basketball player ever. He was named the NBA's Most Valuable Player five times, and he led the league in scoring 10 times. There's no question that he had a lot to do with the Bulls' success.

But Michael could not be a championship team all by himself. Even a player as terrific as Michael needs help. The Bulls did not win any championships until they surrounded Michael with some great players and an excellent coach. Once they got those ingredients, though, they became unstoppa-BULL!

The Bulls were not a good team when Michael joined them for the 1984-85 season. They had had a record of just 27 wins and 55 losses the previous season. With Michael on board, the Bulls improved only to 38–44. Michael played well (he was named NBA Rookie of the Year), but his teammates didn't.

THE TEAM THE BULLS BUILT

Clearly, Michael needed help. The team was rebuilt, season by season. In 1985, the Bulls acquired guard John Paxson. John was known for his deadly outside shooting. Power forward Horace Grant was drafted two years later. The Bulls then traded for small forward Scottie Pippen. Horace gave the Bulls rebounding and toughness. Scottie developed into a great all-around player. Center Bill Cartwright joined the team in a 1988 trade with the New York Knicks. Bill was 7' 1".

The new players made the Bulls a more complete team, but they still came up short in the playoffs. The team finished 47–35 in 1988-89 and made it to the conference finals for the first time since 1975. There, they lost to the Detroit Pistons.

The Bulls continued to improve. In 1989, another strong shooting guard, B.J. Armstrong, became a Bull and Phil Jackson was named head coach. Under Coach Jackson, the

Bulls began to play a style of basketball called the triangle offense. The new offense stressed teamwork and ball movement. The goal was to keep players moving around the court, even when they did not have the ball. The offense allowed more passing so everyone stayed involved in the offense. If everyone was involved, then the Bulls' opponents could not just key on Michael. With Michael, a solid supporting cast, and Phil Jackson's coaching, all the pieces were in place for a championship.

TO THE TOP

By 1990-91, the Bulls were a strong team and they played like it. In the regular season, they raced to a 61–21 record and finished first in the Central Division. In the playoffs, they won the first two rounds easily. They swept the New York Knicks, 3–0, and beat the Philadelphia 76ers, 4–1.

But Chicago faced a familiar opponent in the conference finals: the Detroit Pistons. The Pistons had won the NBA championship two seasons in a row. They had eliminated the Bulls from the playoffs in each of the three previous seasons. They were a tough, strong team. They always played a very physical game against Chicago. Piston center Bill Laimbeer and forward Dennis Rodman were especially rough and were known for doing a lot of bumping and pushing. The Bulls had a hard time with that style of play.

This time, the Bulls were ready for the Pistons. Chicago beat Detroit at its own game by playing tough defense. The triangle offense worked to perfection. Chicago swept Detroit in four games! People who thought of the Bulls as a one-man army had to think again. The Bulls were playing as a team. They were on their way to play the Los Angeles Lakers in their first NBA Finals!

The Bulls lost the first game of the Finals, 93–91, on a last-second shot. But they came back strong in Game 2, charging to a 107–86 win.

After that, the series was all Chicago. The Bulls won the next three games to win the title. Scottie scored 32 points in the final game. John shot an amazing .653 for the series. Michael averaged 31.2 points, 11.4 assists, and 6.6 rebounds a game, and was named the Most Valuable Player. After seven long seasons, Michael and the Bulls had won their first NBA championship! Michael had tears in his eyes.

"After we won the championship in my freshman year [at the University of North Carolina, in 1982], I felt happy, but not all that emotional," said Michael. "But in the pros, I've seen it from the opposite side. All the struggles, all the people saying 'He's not gonna win,' all those little doubts you have about yourself. You have to put them aside and think positive. 'I am gonna win! I'm a winner!' And then

OLYMPIC DREAMS

Michael Jordan and Scottie Pippen won their second NBA championship with the Bulls in 1992. Then they took some time off to play for another terrific team: the Dream Team!

The Dream Team was the best collection of basketball stars ever to play together. The team was put together for the 1992 Summer Olympics, in Barcelona, Spain. That was the first time pro basketball players were allowed to compete on the U.S. Olympic team.

Many of the pros had never played in the Olympics, and they wanted to show basketball fans around the world just how great U.S. basketball could be. Did they ever show them!

Michael and Scottie had amazing teammates: NBA standouts Charles Barkley, Larry Bird, Clyde Drexler, Patrick Ewing, Magic Johnson, Karl Malone, Chris Mullin, David Robinson, and John Stockton, plus college player of the year Christian Laettner.

The Dream Teamers dominated the Olympics. They set an Olympic record by averaging 117 points per game. They won their eight games by an average of 44 points!

The U.S. won the gold medal by beating Croatia, 117–85. For some of the Dream Team players, it was the greatest moment of their basketball careers.

"This shows you're the best," said Scottie. "Nothing means as much to me as having this gold medal."

when you do it, well, it's just amazing." There would be more amazing feats to come.

BETTER AND BETTER

As terrific as the Bulls' 1990-91 season was, the next one was even better! Chicago set a team record with 67 wins during the regular season. Michael averaged 30.1 points per game to lead the league in scoring for the sixth straight season. His teammates were playing better than ever.

The Bulls made the Finals again and met the talented Portland Trail Blazers. Michael's long-distance shooting in Game 1 was remarkable. Eighteen of the 35 points he scored in the first half came from 3-point baskets! The sixth 3-pointer of the half was a new Finals' record. The Bulls won the game, 122–89. They won the Final series in six games for their second straight title.

The Bulls entered the 1992-93 season focused on becoming the first NBA team in 27 seasons to win three straight NBA championships. They started by winning 57 regular-season games and won their third Central Division title in a row. The Bulls breezed through the playoffs and faced the Phoenix Suns in the NBA Finals.

The Bulls won the first two games of the series, but Phoenix won two of the three games in Chicago. The Suns were threatening to tie the series at three games apiece in Game 6. With 14.1 seconds remaining, the Suns were leading, 98–96, but Chicago had the ball. The Bulls called a timeout to plan one last play. What a play it was. All five Bulls touched the ball. It started with Michael throwing the ball in to B.J. and it ended with John Paxson sinking a 3-pointer. The Bulls had won their third straight championship, 99–98! Now that was teamwork!

Michael had averaged a Finals record 41 points per game while collecting his third straight MVP award. It was one of the best performances in a championship series. The Bulls had their "three-peat." But changes were around the corner.

GOOD-BYE AND HELLO!

On October 6, 1993, Michael shocked the world by retiring from basketball. He said he had nothing more to prove and that he had lost his desire to play hoops. The next spring, he played minor league baseball for the Birmingham Barons.

With Michael gone, the Bulls made a number of changes to the team. Over the next two seasons, John Paxson and Bill Cartwright retired. B.J. Armstrong and Horace Grant left to play for other teams.

The Bulls lost some good players, but they replaced them with good players. Guard Ron Harper brought scoring and defense to the squad and guard Steve Kerr replaced John Paxson as the Bulls' best 3-point shooter. Centers Luc Longley and Bill Wennington plugged up the middle, and forward Toni Kukoc *[KOO-coach]* added great shooting and ball-handling skills for a player his size (6' 11"). Scottie was the leader of the Jordanless Bulls, averaging 22 points a game. The team won 55 games in 1993-94, but lost to the New York Knicks in the playoffs.

Then, something happened that made the Bulls — and basketball fans everywhere — very happy. On March 19, 1995, Michael returned to basketball! He had missed the game he loved too much. Michael joined the Bulls for the last 17 games of the regular season and the playoffs. Even with Michael back, the Bulls weren't at their best that season. They lost to the Orlando Magic in the conference semi-finals.

ON THE REBOUND

Chicago looked forward to making a run at its fourth NBA championship in 1995-96. All they needed was one more great player to make the team complete. That player turned out to be one of Chicago's foes from the old Detroit Pistons: Dennis Rodman!

Dennis stood out from the crowd. He had tattoos, and he changed his hair color a lot. He sometimes said and did weird things. But Dennis was a fantastic rebounder and knew how to hustle. The Bulls knew he could help their team, so they acquired him from San Antonio in a trade. With Dennis, the team was ready to make history.

EVERYBODY HELPS

The 1995-96 Bulls were the best NBA team ever! They began the season with 41 wins and only three losses. They went on to set the all-time mark for the best regular-season record, with 72 wins and only 10 losses. Michael was back, big-time! He won his eighth scoring title, with an average of 30.4 points per game. He also won his fourth NBA MVP award.

But, once again, it was Michael's teammates who turned a good team into a great one. Dennis led the league in rebounding with 14.9 per game. Scottie averaged 19.4 points. Toni was honored as the NBA's best Sixth Man (the first player off the bench), while Steve Kerr hit more than half his 3-point shots. (He made 122 of his 237 attempts.)

What made this Chicago team even better than the earlier teams was its great defense. Michael, Scottie, Dennis, and Ron Harper were fantastic defenders. The Bulls were third in the league in defense, allowing only 92.9 points per game.

Chicago met the Seattle SuperSonics in the NBA Finals. The Bulls won the first two games at home, then traveled to Seattle for Game 3. Michael went wild. In the first half, he seemed determined to outscore the entire Sonics team by himself! His 27 points led Chicago to a 62–38 halftime lead. The Bulls won, 108–86.

"That was a spectacular game," Coach Jackson said afterward. "It was one of the best we've played all season and probably our best in the playoffs."

But the Sonics did not give up. Down three games to none, they rallied to win the next two games before the series moved back to Chicago. Game 6, though, was all Bulls. Dennis had 19 rebounds. Scottie scored 17 points. Chicago defeated the Sonics, 87–75.

They had done it! The Bulls were *four-time* NBA champs! Their 72–10 regular-season record, added to their 15–3 playoff record, gave them a total of 87 wins and only 13 losses. Unreal! Everyone knew that Michael was the best ever. Now they knew the Bulls were, too.

HEROIC EFFORT
· ·

These new Bulls weren't done yet. With all their key players back for the 1996-97 season, Chicago marched through the regular season and playoffs to return to the NBA Finals. This time, they played the Utah Jazz. After four games, the series was tied at two games apiece.

Game 5 was played in Salt Lake City, Utah. Michael came

down with a stomach virus before the game. He had a headache and barely enough strength to stand. Could he play? Michael not only played, he put on one of his most memorable performances! He scored 38 points and hit the 3-point shot that gave Chicago an exciting 90–88 victory. Still, Michael had to be helped off the court at one point, because he was so weak.

"Because of the circumstances, with this being a critical game in the Finals, I'd have to say this is the greatest game I've seen Michael play," Coach Jackson said afterward. "Just standing up there . . . caused him dizzy spells. This was a heroic effort, one to add to the collection of efforts that make up his legend." The Bulls had added to their team legend, too, with their fifth NBA title!

Michael, Scottie, Dennis, Toni, Ron, and Coach Jackson were back for another run at the title in 1997-98. Most of them planned to retire or move to other teams when the season ended, so they called the season "The Last Dance." The question was, would it be a Victory Dance?

In the regular season, Chicago won its third straight Central Division title with a 62–20 record. When playoff time came, they kept cruising. They eased past the New Jersey Nets and Charlotte Hornets. Then they edged out the Indiana Pacers to advance to the Finals, where they faced the Jazz once more.

After going up three games to two, the Bulls went back to Utah for Game 6. With 42 seconds left, the Jazz held an 86–83 lead. Would Utah force a seventh game? Would the Bulls give up their title?

THE LAST SHOT

he stage was set for another Michael miracle. He took the ball and raced down the floor. He scored to bring Chicago within 1 point, 86–85.

Utah in-bounded the ball and passed it inside. But Michael reached out and stole it. He dribbled upcourt, where he was met by Jazz defender Bryon Russell. Michael started to drive hard to the basket. Bryon followed. Michael jammed on the brakes and launched a 17-foot jumper with just 5.2 seconds left. *Nothing but net!*

The Bulls won the game, 87–86. The win gave the team its sixth championship in eight seasons! Michael won his sixth Finals MVP award. This was the best finish yet for the best team of the decade.

In January 1999, Michael retired for good. Coach Jackson left basketball to take some time off. Scottie, Dennis, and Steve went to play for other teams. The Bulls' basketball dynasty was over. But the six NBA championships won by Michael and his teammates will always live in the memory of basketball fans everywhere.

7

THE BOSTON CELTICS

The longest-running dynasty in the NBA won 16 championships over 30 years

The Chicago Bulls won six NBA championships in eight seasons. That's an impressive run, but it's nowhere near the best in NBA history. Just check out the Boston Celtics.

The Celtics have won nearly *three* times as many NBA titles as the Bulls! They were NBA champions 16 times from 1956-57 through 1985-86. During one stretch, they won the title 11 times in 13 seasons, including eight in a row (1958-59 to 1965-66)! No other major sports team has dominated a league like that. The Celtics of that era made it look easy, thanks to legendary stars such as center Bill Russell and guards Bob Cousy and Sam Jones.

There's more! In the 1970's, the Celtics won two more NBA titles, with the help of star swingman John Havlicek *[HAV-le-check]*, center Dave Cowens, and guard JoJo White. Then, in the 1980's, forwards Larry Bird and Kevin McHale and center Robert Parish led the Celtics to the NBA crown three more times!

But the Celtic tradition of winning began way back in 1956, when a 22-year-old rookie center named Bill Russell came to Boston.

THE BIG GUY

The Celtics were a good team in the mid-1950's. Then, in 1956, head coach and team vice-president Arnold "Red" Auerbach *[OW-er-back]* traded for center Bill Russell. Bill turned a good team into a *great* one.

Bill changed the way basketball was played. At 6' 10", he was tall, but he was also quick and athletic. Bill was the first to control games with his defense, not with his scoring (although he scored 15 points a game during his career).

Bill led the league in rebounding five times and averaged 22.5 rebounds per game over his 13-season career. In one game, he grabbed 51 rebounds! That's more than entire teams usually get. The 1997-98 Bulls, for example, averaged 44.9 rebounds per game *as a team!* Bill was also the league's first great shot-blocker. He swatted opponents' shots away

We did it! After three Super Bowl losses, John Elway and the Denver Broncos finally won the NFL championship — twice!

The 49ers wouldn't be five-time Super Bowl champs without Jerry Rice. He caught key passes thrown by both Joe Montana and Steve Young.

In the 1990's, Dallas Cowboy running back Emmitt Smith rushed for a Super Bowl record five touchdowns in three wins.

The 1927 New York Yankees *(below)* and the 1998 Yankees earned ticker-tape parades in New York City for winning the World Series. The '98 team won more games than any team ever.

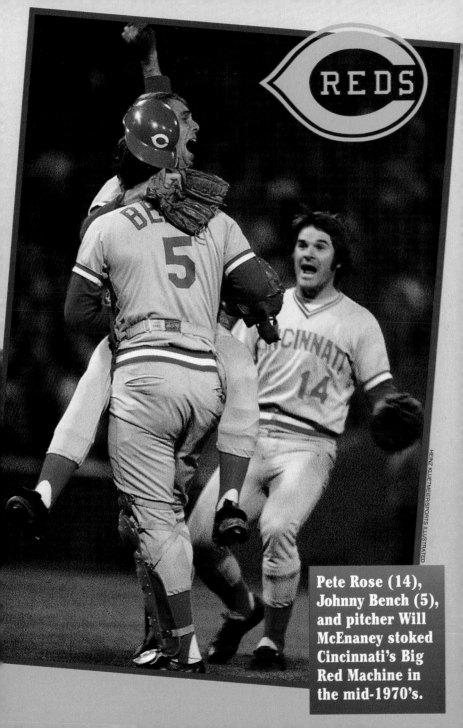

REDS

Pete Rose (14), Johnny Bench (5), and pitcher Will McEnaney stoked Cincinnati's Big Red Machine in the mid-1970's.

Celtic center Bill Russell helped his team win many of those championship banners seen hanging on high in Boston Garden.

In 1998, this herd of famous Bulls celebrated Chicago's sixth title in eight seasons. Then they went their separate ways.

ANDREW D. BERNSTEIN/NBA PHOTOS

HEINZ KLUETMEIER/SPORTS ILLUSTRATED

Chamique Holdsclaw (23) led Tennessee's Lady Vols to three straight NCAA titles, starting in 1996.

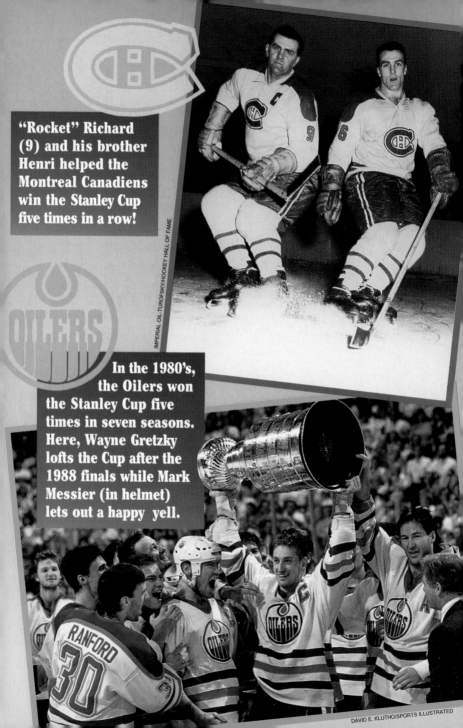

"Rocket" Richard (9) and his brother Henri helped the Montreal Canadiens win the Stanley Cup five times in a row!

In the 1980's, the Oilers won the Stanley Cup five times in seven seasons. Here, Wayne Gretzky lofts the Cup after the 1988 finals while Mark Messier (in helmet) lets out a happy yell.

from the basket — and often into teammates' hands.

In his very first season (1956-57), Bill led the Celtics to the NBA Finals, where they met the powerful St. Louis Hawks. The Series went to a winner-take-all Game 7. And that game went to double overtime! The Celtics won their first NBA title, 125–123. Bill averaged 22.9 rebounds in the series and grabbed 32 of them in the Game 7 victory.

The Celtics lost to St. Louis in the Finals the following season, but came back to win the first of eight championships in a row in 1959. The Philadelphia 76ers ended the Celtic streak in 1967.

Bill was named Boston's head coach in 1966. With Bill leading the team as a player-coach, they won back-to-back championships in 1968 and 1969!

TERRIFIC TEAMMATES

Bill had a lot of great teammates. "At one time," said Bill, "we had four guys playing guard on our team, and they all went to the Hall of Fame." Bill was talking about the 1960-61 team, which included Bob Cousy, Bill Sharman, Sam Jones, and K.C. Jones. The most famous was Bob, who played for the Celtics from 1950-51 to 1962-63.

Bob was one of the first true point guards. A point guard's job is to bring the ball upcourt, set up his teammates, and direct the offense. Nobody played the position like Bob. He was a terrific ball handler and dribbler and a great passer.

It wasn't just that Bob passed the ball — it was the way he passed it. He used behind-the-back passes and no-look passes to confuse opponents. He led the league in assists for eight straight seasons.

Bob could score too! He averaged 18.4 points per game during his career. "Cousy didn't really become great until his third season with the Celtics," Coach Auerbach wrote in his autobiography, *Red Auerbach*. "After that, he was the best I ever saw."

Bill Sharman was a starting guard for the Celtics from 1952-53 to 1960-61. He averaged 17.8 points per game and shot 88 percent from the free-throw line during his 11-season career. He once sank 55 free throws in a row!

CELTICS CHAMPIONSHIP YEARS

1956-57	1963-64	1975-76
1958-59	1964-65	1980-81
1959-60	1965-66	1983-84
1960-61	1967-68	1985-86
1961-62	1968-69	
1962-63	1973-74	

When Bob and Bill retired, backup guards Sam Jones and K.C. Jones took over, and the Celtics didn't miss a beat. Sam averaged 17.7 points per game in his 12 seasons. He also introduced the bank shot to the NBA. (A bank shot is a shot that hits the backboard before going into the basket.)

K.C. Jones was an expert defender who was usually matched against the opposing team's better guard. His smothering defense allowed other Celtic guards to concentrate on scoring and passing. The two Joneses (they were not related) played their way into the Hall of Fame.

The talent on those 1960's Celtics teams did not end there. John Havlicek played guard and forward from 1962-63 to 1977-78. He averaged 20.8 points a game over 16 seasons. Tom "Satch" Sanders was one of the best defensive forwards in the league. Tom Heinsohn was a tough, offensive rebounder who also averaged 18.6 points per game. Forward Bailey Howell, who averaged nearly 19 points a game during his career, added more scoring punch for Boston's last two title teams of the decade.

THE MASTERMIND

How did Coach Auerbach end up with all that talent? "Red recruited very wisely," Sam said. "He only chose players from winning college programs."

Coach Auerbach was also a master at getting the most

THE LEGENDARY LAKERS

No team has been to the NBA Finals more often than the Lakers. They have played in the NBA's championship series 24 times! They have won 11 championships. Only the Boston Celtics have won more titles (16).

The Lakers are a legendary team, with a history of fantastic players. But the Lakers legend didn't begin in Los Angeles. The Lakers started out in Minneapolis, Minnesota. The team was founded in 1948, just two years after the NBA was formed.

The Minneapolis Lakers were basketball's first dynasty. From 1949 to 1954, they won five championships. George Mikan was the team's biggest star. He was 6' 10". George was the first big man to star in the NBA.

The Lakers moved to Los Angeles, California, in 1960. They won five championships from 1980 through 1988. Standout players who helped the Los Angeles Lakers included centers Wilt Chamberlain and Kareem Abdul-Jabbar; forward Elgin Baylor; and guards Jerry West and Magic Johnson. Jerry and Elgin led the Lakers to seven NBA Finals in nine years, from 1962 to 1970. Wilt helped Los Angeles win its first NBA title, in 1972. Kareem and Magic helped the Lakers become the first team in 19 years to repeat as NBA champions, in 1987 and 1988.

out of his players. "We were always in great shape," said Sam. "We were well-briefed. We knew in detail the strengths and weaknesses of all opponents."

Coach Auerbach kept his teams well-prepared because he hated to lose. He was very competitive, even off the court. "He'd foam at the mouth even when he was playing racquetball," K.C. said. "With him and Russell, you had that dislike for losing straight at the top and coming right down through everyone."

Boston's style of play was simple: It was fast. The Celtics were the first NBA team to play "fast-break basketball." As soon as they got the ball, they ran it upcourt before the other team could set up its defense.

"We used to run with wild abandon," said Bob Cousy. "In Auerbach's mind, if we went a full 48 minutes without ever calling a play, that was the ultimate success."

The more Boston ran, the less teams were able to stop them. And it got so the Celtics were always running. "We didn't have to think much about it," said Sam Jones. "We just did it. And every time we did, you could see the fear in the other team's eyes."

The only team the Celtics couldn't scare off was the Philadelphia 76ers and their powerful center, Wilt Chamberlain. (But they still beat the Sixers a lot.) The teams met in the Eastern Division finals four times.

Boston won three times. Wilt and his teammates always had trouble winning in the famous Boston Garden, which is where the Celtics played until the 1995-96 season.

"It was like being in a Roman amphitheater and you were one of the Christians being fed to the lions," Wilt once said of playing in front of the hostile Boston crowds.

Bill Russell retired as player-coach in 1969. Tom Heinsohn took over as head coach and led Boston to the NBA championship in 1974 and 1976. John Havlicek's winning ways and versatile talent led that team, which had another strong group of players. Center Dave Cowens and forward Paul Silas fought inside for rebounds and points while speedy JoJo White lit up the scoreboard with his outside shooting.

LARRY TO THE RESCUE

By 1978-79, though, Boston's record had sunk to 29–53, the second worst in the league. Was the Celtic magic gone? No way! Help came soon, in the form of a gawky forward from French Lick, Indiana, named Larry Bird.

Larry had been a star at Indiana State University. He led the little-known school all the way to the NCAA Championship Game. He helped turn the Celtics around immediately when he joined the team for the 1979-80 season. Boston finished with a 61–21 record, and Larry was named the NBA Rookie of the Year!

The next season, center Robert "Chief" Parish and power forward Kevin McHale joined the team. The Celtics were ready to battle for the NBA title again — and battle they did, winning championships in 1981, 1984, and 1986.

Larry was one of the best all-around players basketball had ever seen. Although he was slow and couldn't jump high, it seemed as if he could score whenever he wanted to. He led the league in free-throw shooting four times. Larry was also a great rebounder and made no-look passes that stunned opponents. He was named the NBA MVP three seasons in a row, from 1983-84 through 1985-86.

But Larry also had great teammates. Robert and Kevin were big, strong guys who could score inside. They also played tough defense and fought for rebounds. Boston also had talented guards. Dennis "D.J." Johnson was a superb ball handler and defensive player. Danny Ainge was a great long-distance shooter. Together, they formed a top team.

In 1992, Larry retired with a bad back. He finished with career averages of 24.3 points, 10 rebounds, and 6.3 assists per game. He became the Indiana Pacers coach in 1997.

But Larry is best known for bringing championship basketball back to Boston, carrying on the tradition that started decades earlier.

8
TENNESSEE LADY VOLUNTEERS

• • • • • • • • • • • • • • • • •

Three NCAA championships in a row gave this team its place in history

The 1994-95 University of Tennessee women's basketball team was loaded with talent. The Lady Volunteers, as they are called, had strong players at every position, more talented players on the bench, and a terrific coach. The Lady Vols won their third straight regular-season conference championship. But they did not win the NCAA championship. In the final game, Rebecca Lobo and her University of Connecticut teammates beat Tennessee, 70–64.

That would not happen again soon. Tennessee turned the disappointing ending of the 1994-95 season into a brand new beginning. The next fall, a 6' 2" freshman named Chamique *[sha-MEE-kwah]* Holdsclaw arrived. The Lady Vols embraced this young star and renewed their determination. Then they went out and became the first team in women's college basketball history to win three NCAA titles in a row!

TEAM HOLDSCLAW

Chamique was a winner, even before she arrived at Tennessee. She had led her high school to four straight New York state championships. Before that, she had led her eighth-grade team to a league championship in Queens, New York! Chamique *knew* how to win titles.

Another person who knew how to win titles was Tennessee coach Pat Summitt. Coach Summitt had already won three championships with the Lady Vols (1987, 1989, and 1991). But after losing the 1995 title game and three top seniors, could she get her team back to its winning ways? And could a rookie like Chamique lead them there?

The answer to both questions was *yes!* Chamique stormed onto the college scene. She averaged 16.2 points and 9.1 rebounds per game for the season. Chamique was good.

Tennessee's veteran players were shocked by just *how* good young Chamique was. Her ball-handling abilities, rebounding, and soft, accurate shot made her dangerous. What was even more impressive was her court presence.

"She's very competitive, very intense, but she has this composure," said Michelle Marciniak, who was a senior in

1995-96. "From a freshman, I couldn't believe it. We could draw confidence from her."

Chamique wasn't the only talented Tennessee player. When the team met the University of Georgia in the 1996 NCAA championship game, many players contributed. Yes, Chamique scored 16 points and had 14 rebounds, but sophomore center Tiffani Johnson also scored 16 points and junior forward Abby Conklin finished with 14 points. At guard, senior Latina Davis played airtight defense and Michelle directed the offense, scored 10 points, and had five assists. Tennessee won easily, 83–65. Michelle was named the tournament's Most Outstanding Player. But Tennessee was just getting started.

SIMPLY UNSTOPPABLE

Despite the graduation of Michelle and Latina, the Lady Vols had high hopes for the 1996-97 season, thanks to Chamique's strength. But injuries and a difficult schedule took their toll. At one point in early January, the team had an unimpressive 10–6 record.

Then, the Lady Vols turned it around. They won 13 of their next 17 games heading into the NCAA tournament. In the Midwest Regional final, they met the top-ranked University of Connecticut. Connecticut had beaten Tennessee, 72–57, during the regular season. This game was different. The

Lady Vols stunned UConn, 91–81, to return to the Final Four.

That's where Chamique took over. In two games, she had a total of 55 points, 12 rebounds, and 6 assists. The Lady Vols crushed the University of Notre Dame, 80–66, in the semifinal and then beat Old Dominion University, 68–59. Tennessee had become only the second women's basketball team to win two straight NCAA championships! (The University of Southern California was the first.)

Chamique had proved she was a superstar. But the Lady Vols, as a team, had also proved something else. They proved that they had heart. All season long, they had faced big challenges — injuries and defeats. They still came out on top. "This team always finds a way to win," said backup point guard Laurie Milligan. "Other teams may be better, but they have to have a bigger heart than we do to beat us."

BETTER THAN EVER

While Tennessee's two championship teams had been great, the 1997-98 Lady Vols were even greater. From the moment the season began, they dominated everyone and everything in their path. They won every single one of their games — 39 in all. That set an NCAA basketball record for victories in one season. And they won those games by an average of *30 points* per game!

Part of Tennessee's tremendous success was due to the

new group of talented freshmen who had joined the team. Forward Tamika Catchings, center Teresa Geter, and guards Semeka Randall and Kristen Clement gave the team skilled players and depth at every position.

How skilled were these freshmen? Tamika averaged more

TOP COMETS

While the Lady Vols were dominating the women's college game, another team emerged as the Top Team in women's professional basketball. The Houston Comets won the first two championships in the brand new Women's National Basketball Association (WNBA).

In 1997, the Comets beat the New York Liberty, 65–51, in the championship game. In 1998, Houston dominated the league, with a sizzling 27–3 regular-season record. Guard Cynthia Cooper averaged 22.7 points per game to claim her second straight MVP award. Forward Sheryl Swoopes was a triple threat on the court, averaging 15.6 points, 5.1 rebounds, and 2.1 assists.

In the playoffs, the Comets swept the Charlotte Sting, 2–0, in the semi-finals. Then, they defeated the Phoenix Mercury, two games to one, to win the title again.

You could say these Comets really soared!

points (18.2 per game), assists (2.4), steals (2.6), and blocks (1.6) than even Chamique had as a freshman! The 6' 1" forward also had a better shooting percentage and fewer turnovers. Semeka averaged 16 points per game.

By this time, Chamique was not only the best player on her team, but clearly the best player in the country and, perhaps, the best college women's player ever! She averaged 23.5 points per game, 8.4 rebounds, and 3 assists during the 1997-98 season. Even her defense had become first-rate.

"Everyone in the country knows I can score," said Chamique. "I figured, I'm quick, big, athletic, and I know I can stop someone. When I see all these players around me — even those that aren't as gifted athletically as I am — go out there and play great defense, I say, 'Mique, you've got to pick it up a little bit. You can't have any weakness in your game.'"

MAKING HISTORY
. . . .

In the 1998 NCAA championship game, Chamique, the fantastic freshmen, and the other Lady Vols put on one of the greatest shows in women's basketball history. They demolished Louisana Tech, 93–75.

Chamique was brilliant, scoring 25 points to go along with 10 rebounds and 6 assists. She was named Most

Outstanding Player of the Final Four for the second straight year. "She wasn't going to let anybody take that championship home except Tennessee," Semeka said of Chamique.

It was Chamique's eighth championship season in a row. More important, it was Tennessee's third straight NCAA title. No women's college basketball team had ever won three NCAA titles in a row. The 1997-98 Lady Vols were being called the best women's team of all-time, and lots of people agreed.

THE STREAK ENDS

The Lady Vols' winning streak continued into the 1998-99 season. They won 46 games in a row before Purdue stopped them, 78–68, in November. They finished the regular season with a 28–2 record. But in the NCAA tournament, Tennessee met a hot team from Duke University and was upset, 69–63, in the NCAA East Regional final.

Chamique finished her four-year career with 3,025 points and 1,295 rebounds, both all-time Tennessee records. She was named the national player of the year twice and was an All-America four times. With Chamique, the Lady Vols had a stunning 131–17 overall record and a 21–1 mark in NCAA tournament play. They had made history.

THE MONTREAL CANADIENS

• •

With more Stanley Cup titles than any other team, they defined hockey greatness

How do you spell hockey excellence? For National Hockey League fans and historians, the answer is C-A-N-A-D-I-E-N-S.

The Montreal Canadiens have won the Stanley Cup a record 24 times (23 of those for the NHL championship, one the year *before* the NHL was started). No other team has won more than 11 Cups. Talk about dynasties! Montreal won five titles in a row once, four in a row another time, and back-to-back championships three other times! The team has won titles in every decade, starting in 1916. Among major sports teams, only baseball's New York Yankees *(see page 34)* has been so successful over such a long period of time.

Montreal is in the province of Quebec, Canada. In Canada for many years, there were no pro baseball or football teams. Hockey was *the* sport. And its players were considered to be heroes. Over the years, 40 of those Montreal heroes have made it to the Hockey Hall of Fame.

STAR POWER

he Canadiens were founded on December 4, 1909. Seven years later, they defeated the Portland (Oregon) Rosebuds to win their first Stanley Cup championship. The NHL didn't even exist yet! One of the great players on that team was goaltender Georges Vezina. The trophy that is now awarded to the league's best goaltender each year is named after Georges. Didier Pitre was another Montreal star. He scored 210 goals in 243 regular-season games over his 20-year career.

But Montreal's first superstar arrived in 1923. His name was Howie Morenz. At only 5' 9", Howie was small for a hockey player, but he was very fast. The fiery center led the league in scoring twice and was named the NHL's Most Valuable Player three times. Howie helped the Canadiens win the Stanley Cup in his first season and led them to back-to-back titles in 1929-30 and 1930-31.

Montreal's next great star was Maurice Richard *[more-REESE ree-SHARD]*. Maurice helped the Canadiens win eight Stanley Cups during his 18-season career. He won one MVP award, played on 14 NHL All-Star teams, and became Montreal's all-time leading goal scorer, with 544 goals.

Maurice's desire and determination were second to no one's. As Maurice said himself, "There were always players who were better — they just didn't work as hard." At 5' 10", Maurice was not big, but he had great speed. Maurice became known as Rocket Richard, or simply "the Rocket."

Maurice had shown promise in the junior hockey leagues, but was often injured. The Canadiens took a chance and brought him up to the NHL in 1942. Maurice responded by getting five goals and six assists in his first 16 games. Then he broke his ankle.

In 1943-44, Maurice led the Canadiens with 32 goals, even though he missed a few games with a shoulder injury. There was a reason for his success. Coach Dick Irvin had moved Maurice to right wing and put him on a line with center Elmer Lach and left wing Toe Blake. It was a terrific combination. Elmer, Toe, and Maurice were so strong and physical that the line they formed became known as the "Punch Line."

"Elmer was good in the corners, and he used to get the defense all mad at him and then they would forget to pay attention to me," Maurice said in an interview in 1996. "Toe liked to go into the corners, too. I had two guys who worked in the corners — I just had to go to the net."

TERRIFIC TORONTO

Besides the Canadiens, only one hockey team has reached double digits when it comes to Stanley Cup championships. The Toronto Maple Leafs have won 11. That may surprise you, since the last Cup they won came in 1967!

It has been awhile since the Maple Leafs were a great team, but what a team they were! From 1942 through 1951, Toronto won six Stanley Cups. The first of those wins was the most dramatic. The Maple Leafs faced the Detroit Red Wings in the finals and lost the first three games in the best-of-seven series. Led by center Syl Apps and goaltender Turk Broda, though, the Leafs stunned everyone by rallying to win the next four games and take the Cup. They are still the only team in NHL finals history to come back to win after being three games down.

That was a great team, but the Toronto teams of the 1960's may have been even better. They won four championships between 1962 and 1967, including three straight from 1962 to 1964. In an era when most teams stayed with the same players from the beginning of their careers on, Maple Leaf manager Punch Imlach did it differently. He brought together an exciting blend of established veterans, including some from other teams, and new talents. His mix was a successful one.

The Canadiens plowed through the 1944 playoffs to win another Cup. The Punch Line scored 21 goals in nine games! Maurice had 12 of those goals. And he didn't get hurt! Rocket kept working, and Montreal kept winning. In 1944-45, Rocket became the first player to score 50 goals in a 50-game season. Montreal finished the regular season in first place but lost in the semi-finals of the Stanley Cup playoffs. A year later, Rocket led Montreal to its sixth championship. The team won the Stanley Cup again in 1952-53. But that was nothing compared to what it would do a few years later.

The Canadiens were about to make history.

THE BEST TEAM EVER

Starting with the 1955-56 season, Montreal won five NHL championships in a row! That is something no other team has ever done. How did they do it? With the greatest team of hockey talent the league has ever seen. These Canadiens had no weaknesses. They had great players at every single position. Rocket led the way on offense, of course. But there were others.

Center Jean *[zhan]* Béliveau was big (6' 3") and graceful. He could score or pass with the very best and finished his 20-season career with 507 goals and 712 assists. His 1,219 points are the second-highest total among all Canadien players. Jean was twice named the league's MVP, in 1956 and 1964, and won the Conn Smythe Award as the 1965 playoff MVP.

"He had an overflow of talent," said teammate Ted Johnson. "There have been great center icemen since him, but no one with the same style. He stands apart for me."

Another trio of offensive standouts were right wing Bernard "Boom Boom" Geoffrion, left wing Dickie Moore, and center Henri Richard, Maurice's younger brother. Boom Boom and Dickie both led the league in scoring twice. "Dickie was slick and tough," Ted Johnson said. "He led the league once [in scoring] even though he had a broken hand." Henri, who was known as "The Pocket Rocket," set an NHL record as well. He won more Stanley Cups than any other player ever: 11!

Montreal's offense was so good that the league changed the power-play rule because of it. According to the old rule, when a player committed a penalty, he had to sit in the penalty box for two full minutes (the length of the penalty), even if the other team scored. That meant the other team had a one-man advantage for two minutes no matter how many goals it scored. The Canadiens scored too many goals with that advantage! In 1956, the NHL changed the rule so that once the team with the advantage scored, the player could leave the penalty box.

"We were the reason they changed the rule," said Ted. "I remember, it was a game against Boston in which Beliveau scored three goals on one power play. Lynn Patrick, who was running the Bruins in those days, was on the [NHL] Board of Governors, and that's when they changed the rule."

DYNAMIC DEFENSE

On defense, the Canadiens were just as solid. Ted Johnson won the Norris Trophy, in 1959, as the league's best defenseman. But he wasn't the best defenseman on his own team! Montreal's Doug Harvey won the Norris Trophy six times in seven years, between 1955 and 1961. The only year in that stretch that he did not win it was the time Ted won it.

The Montreal defense took pride in shutting down other teams. "We had two goals every year," Ted said. "Win as many games as possible, and make sure our goaltender won the Vezina Trophy." Mission accomplished! Goalie Jacques Plante won the Vezina Trophy (at the time, it was for giving up the fewest goals) six times. During the Canadiens' championship streak, he won it five times in a row!

Jacques made his mark on the game in another important way. On November 1, 1959, he became the first NHL goaltender to wear a mask to protect his face in a game. Not only did the mask protect him from injury, but it also helped him keep the puck out of the net. "When I'm sprawled out on the ice," Jacques said, "I can actually stop the puck with it. It's like having another hand." Soon, every goalie started wearing a mask.

Eleven Montreal players from that era were elected to the Hockey Hall of Fame. "I remember being young in this league and asking Red Storey, the old referee, 'Why are we so good?' " Ted remembered. "He said, 'Make up a list of the Top 10 players in the league. Six or seven of them are on your team.' "

POST-ROCKET POWER

In 1960, the Canadiens swept the Chicago Blackhawks and the Toronto Maple Leafs to win its fifth straight Cup. They were as dominant as ever, giving up only 11 goals in those eight playoff games.

But the championship series marked the end for Rocket Richard. After one of his goals against Toronto, he skated back to pick up the puck as a keepsake. That told the world that he was planning to retire. Before the next season, he did just that.

Would the Canadiens be able to win a title without the Rocket? For a few years, the answer seemed to be no. Montreal lost in the playoff semi-finals four straight years after Rocket retired. But then the team broke through, and in a big way. From 1965 through 1971, the Canadiens won five Stanley Cups in seven seasons. Only two other NHL teams have matched that: the Toronto Maple Leafs, in 1944-51 *(see page 82)*, and the Edmonton Oilers, in 1983-90 *(see page 89)*.

While Rocket had been the leader of the 1950's teams, now Jean was running the show. His goal-scoring, combined with the defense of Jacques Laperrière and the goaltending of Gump Worsley, made Montreal as dangerous as ever. And they knew it. "We always started the year on a positive note, thinking we would win," said Jean. And they usually did.

After Jean led the team to the Stanley Cup in 1971, he, too, retired. Not to worry: Another talented player arrived in 1971-72 to keep Montreal on top. Guy Lafleur *[ghee la-FLUR]* was a rightwinger with terrific speed and instincts and a great scoring touch. Guy led the NHL in scoring for three straight seasons and was named the league's Most Valuable Player in 1977 and 1978. He went on to become the all-time Canadien leader in assists, with 728, and points, with 1,246.

Balancing Guy's offensive skills were the outstanding goaltending skills of Ken Dryden. Ken won the Vezina Trophy five years in a row, starting in 1973. Together, Guy and Ken sparked Montreal to five more Stanley Cups, including four in a row from 1976-79. Once again, the Canadiens dominated the league.

Playing alongside these two were such outstanding players as Yvan Cournoyer, Jacques Lemaire, and Larry Robinson. Yvan, a quick right wing, sped to 10 Stanley Cup titles between 1964 and 1979. Jacques was one of the best all-around centers in the league. He played for eight Stanley Cup champions between 1968 and 1979. He scored the Cup-winning goals in 1977 and 1979. Larry was one of the best defensemen in NHL history and set an NHL record by being in the playoffs for 20 years in a row!

Top teams need top coaches, and these Montreal teams had one in Scotty Bowman. He led the Canadiens to five Stanley Cups in eight seasons. He left Montreal after its fourth Stanley Cup in a row, in 1979. Then he went on to win more Cups as the coach of the Pittsburgh Penguins and Detroit Red Wings!

But the Canadiens weren't done just yet. In 1986, a lanky rookie goalie named Patrick Roy *[wah]* got so hot during the playoffs that he made Montreal a champion again! Seven years later, Patrick led Montreal to the 1993 Stanley Cup championship with another awesome performance.

That brought the Canadiens' total number of Stanley Cup titles to 24. No other team has won even *half* that amount! The 1993 win also made the Canadiens the only major pro sports team to win a league championship in nine straight decades. Now they are aiming for the next millennium! ♆

10

THE EDMONTON OILERS

· · · · · · · · · · · · · · · ·

The game's best player and terrific teammates lit up rinks with scoring power

Offensive firepower — the ability to score goals almost at will — set the 1980's Edmonton Oilers apart from other great hockey teams. That, and a player named Wayne Gretzky. Wayne, who retired from the NHL in April 1999, was the best player in hockey history. During his 20-year NHL career, he set an eye-popping 61 records. Those records include most goals (894), assists (1,963), and points (2,857) in a career.

Wayne was at his best in the early '80s, when he played for the Oilers. And Wayne made players around him play their best. He did it by setting an example of hard work and passion for the game. He also did it by passing the puck to a teammate — usually just at the right time to allow that player to score a goal. Wayne passed the puck better than anyone who ever laced up a pair of skates.

But even The Great One, as Wayne was called, had to have someone to pass the puck to. That was no problem on those Edmonton teams! Mark Messier, Paul Coffey, Glenn Anderson, Jari Kurri, and a slew of other young stars were all too happy to help out. Together, this team won four Stanley Cup championships in five years, from 1984 through 1988. Then, the Oilers won a fifth Cup, in 1990, without Wayne. That proved what most hockey fans and experts already knew: The Oilers were never a one-player team.

WELCOME TO THE NHL

When Wayne joined the Edmonton Oilers, the team wasn't even a part of the NHL. Edmonton played in the World Hockey Association (WHA). The WHA was founded in 1972. Its teams signed a few big NHL stars, such as Hall of Famer Bobby Hull, and found a lot of young talent as it tried to create a strong, new league. Wayne was one of those young talents.

In 1979, the WHA merged with the NHL. Only four WHA teams, including the Oilers, were accepted into the NHL.

Whatever league they were in, the Oilers knew they had the best player. They soon surrounded him with other excellent players. In the 1979 NHL draft, Edmonton picked up two outstanding skaters, center Mark Messier *[MEHS-ey-ay]* and right wing Glenn Anderson.

Unlike Wayne, Mark relied on strength and toughness. At 6' 1" and 205 pounds, he was never afraid to use his muscle to his advantage. But Mark wasn't just a tough guy. He was a fast skater and fine scorer. Glenn was a lightning-fast skater, too. He scored 50 or more goals in a season twice during his career.

In 1980, the Oilers selected defenseman Paul Coffey and right wing Jari Kurri *[YAH-ree KOOR-ee]* in the draft. Paul was an "offensive defenseman." He set NHL records for most career goals, assists, and points by a defenseman. In 1985-86, he scored 48 goals, the most ever in one season by a defenseman! Jari was a goal-scoring machine. He was especially good in the playoffs. In 1985, he tied the NHL record for most goals in one playoff season, with 19. (He retired in 1998 with 106 playoff goals.)

The Oilers had plenty of scoring ability now. What they needed was someone to stop their opponents from scoring. They found that person at the 1981 draft: goalie Grant Fuhr *[FYOOR]*. Grant was a big, strong guy with quick reflexes. He quickly became the best goalie in the NHL and remained on top for most of the 1980's.

By 1984, the Oilers were more than ready to make a run

MIRACLE ON ICE

The most memorable moment in U.S. hockey history happened not in the NHL, but in the Olympics. At the 1980 Winter Olympics, in Lake Placid, New York, Team USA faced the team from the Soviet Union. Before 1991, Russia and 14 smaller republics formed a powerful country called the Soviet Union. In world politics, the U.S. and Soviet Union were big rivals.

On the ice, the Soviets had won the four previous Olympic gold medals. The U.S. team was not expected to win any kind of medal. Pro players were not allowed on the team at the time, so it was made up mostly of young, inexperienced college kids.

The two teams met in the semi-finals. The Soviets took leads twice in the first period, but the U.S. evened the score both times. Through two periods, the Soviets had outshot the Americans, 30–10. They led only 3–2 because of great goaltending by Team USA's Jim Craig. In the third period, Mark Johnson of the U.S. scored his second goal of the game to even the score at 3.

Then, with 10 minutes left in the game, team captain Mike Eruzione *[ur-ROOS-ee-OWN-ee]* fired the game-winner. Team USA shocked the world by winning, 4–3. Two days later, the U.S. defeated Finland, 4–2, to capture the gold and the hearts of all Americans.

for the Stanley Cup. But they had to get by the New York Islanders. The Islanders had eliminated Edmonton in the quarterfinals of the playoffs in 1981. In the 1983 Stanley Cup Finals, they had swept the Oilers in four games.

OFFENSIVE OILERS

The two teams met in the Stanley Cup Finals again in 1984. The Oilers won two of the first three games, but the Islanders were still confident.

Oiler coach Glen Sather *[SAY-thur]* wasn't worried either. Before Game 4, he boldly predicted that the Islanders would not win another game. They didn't! Edmonton overwhelmed them, scoring a stunning 19 goals in the final three games. The Oilers had won their first Stanley Cup. Mark had scored 26 points in 19 games. He was awarded the Conn Smythe Trophy as MVP of the play-offs. Wayne had scored 13 goals and made 22 assists. The Oilers were still young (their average age was 26) and fun-loving. But the dynasty had begun.

The next season, the Oilers went 49-20-11 in the regular season. They lost only three playoff games on the way to their second straight championship. Wayne set an NHL playoff record with 47 points in 18 games and won his first Conn Smythe Trophy. The question now was, could the Oilers make it three straight?

When the 1986 playoffs began, the Oilers seemed certain to win their third straight title. They had just completed the regular season with a 56-17-7 record. Three of the top four scorers in the NHL were Oilers! What could possibly go wrong in the playoffs?

In the first round, the answer was nothing. Edmonton swept the Vancouver Canucks in three straight games, outscoring them 17–5. In the Smythe Division final, the Oilers faced their big rivals, the Calgary Flames. (Calgary and Edmonton are located in the same province of Canada, Alberta.) The teams split the first six games. Everything came down to Game 7. The winner would advance to the next round. The loser would go home for the season.

The game was tied, 2–2, with five minutes left in the third period. Then, disaster struck the Oilers. Edmonton defenseman Steve Smith got the puck behind his own net and tried to shoot it out of the Oilers' zone. But his pass hit the back of goalie Grant Fuhr's leg and landed in Edmonton's own goal! Calgary won, 3–2. The Oilers' season was over.

Could it be that Edmonton's "dynasty" was crumbling already? After a 4–4 start in the 1986-87 season, the Oilers came together. They had a 50-24-6 season and then cruised through the playoffs. In the finals, they battled a tough Philadelphia Flyer team through seven games to win their third Stanley Cup. Nobody was happier than Steve, whose deflected pass into his own net had cost the Oilers so dearly the year before. Afterward, Wayne summed up Edmonton's third title well: "The Oilers proved that their hockey — emphasizing speed, offense, skating — is the kind of hockey that wins Stanley Cup championships."

To prove he was right, Edmonton went out in 1987-88 and did it all again! Grant had his best season. He won a career-best 40 games and was awarded the Vezina Trophy as the NHL's best goalie.

For the first time since 1980-81, the Oilers did not finish first in their division. They finished second, behind Calgary. It didn't matter. Once the playoffs started, the Oilers didn't mess around. They lost only two games in four rounds to claim their fourth championship in five seasons. In the Stanley Cup Finals, they swept the Boston Bruins.

WAYNE-LESS WORLD
. . . .

Even as Oiler fans were still celebrating, the unthinkable happened. Wayne left Edmonton! The Oilers traded him to the Los Angeles Kings for money, players, and draft picks before the 1988-89 season. Fans were outraged. But Edmonton owner Peter Pocklington believed that the Oilers needed more money to remain in business. He got it: He sent Wayne and others to Los Angeles for a package of players and $15 million! To add insult to injury, Wayne's Kings defeated Edmonton in the first round of the 1989 playoffs!

By the time the 1990 playoffs rolled around, only seven players remained from the Oilers' first championship club. Wayne was in L.A., and Paul Coffey was playing for Pittsburgh. Grant had been sidelined by a shoulder injury. But one of those remaining players was Mark Messier, and he was playing better than ever.

Edmonton squeaked by the Winnipeg Jets in the first round, four games to three, and then met up with Wayne's Kings in Round 2. This time there were no surprises. The Oilers scored 24 goals in four games and swept Los Angeles.

After beating Chicago in six games in the next round, the Oilers were back in the finals, facing the Boston Bruins. Could the Oilers win it all without Wayne? They could, and did! Boston won just one game in the finals.

The Oilers had skated to another title. It was their fifth Stanley Cup trophy in seven years! Only two other teams had ever done that: the Montreal Canadiens *(see page 79)* and the Toronto Maple Leafs *(see page 82)*.

But Edmonton had done it by playing the most exciting brand of hockey the league had ever seen. Teams in the future may come along and win lots of NHL titles, but none are likely to score as much or be as much fun to watch as the Edmonton Oilers of the 1980's.